MW00737391

THE EXILE HOUSE

Erling Friis-Baastad

salmonpoetry

Published in 2001 by
Salmon Publishing Ltd,
Cliffs of Moher, Co. Clare, Ireland
http://www.salmonpoetry.com
email: info@salmonpoetry.com

ISBN 1 903392 14 4   Paperback

Cover photography by Ilsa Thielan
Cover design & typesetting by Siobhán Hutson
Printed by Offset Paperback Mfrs., Inc., PA

For my mother

Acknowledgements

Some of the these have previously appeared in the following magazines: *Blue Jacket* (Japan), *The Carrionflower Writ* (Australia), *Cross-Country*, *Dog River Review*, *ICE-FLOE*, *The Malahat Review*, *The Northern Review*, *Northward Journal*, *Poetry Canada*, *Poetry Toronto*.

Many of these poems have also appeared in chapbooks: *The Ash Lad* and *Cendrars' Hand* (Alpha Beat Press); *The Exile House* (Beginner's Mind Press); *The Laws of Gravity* (Reference West/The Hawthorne Society). Others have appeared in the anthologies *Writing North* (Beluga Books), *Because You Loved Being A Stranger* (Harbour Publishing), *Insights: Cultures* (Harcourt Brace Canada Ltd.) and *Up from the Permafrost* (Yukon Learn). My thanks to all the editors for their encouragement.

I would also like to thank Lotteries Yukon and the Yukon government's Arts Branch for two Advanced Artist Awards which helped make this book a reality.

I deeply appreciate poet Brian Brett's wise editing suggestions.

My love and gratitude to my companion Patricia Robertson for everything, including editing.

Contents

I

Portraits Of A Lady 3
What We Don't Yet Know About Uncles 4
Filialis 5
A Heritage 6
The Ash Lad 7
On Vilano Bridge 9
Better Than Nothing 10
Whenever I See You Now, You're Laughing 11
The Strait 12
Badlands Jesus 14
Writing The Novel 16
The Poet Attempts A Novel 17
Like Love 18
The Exile House 19

II

The Death Of Saint-Denys Garneau 23
Sedimentary 24
Here, Now 25
The Laws Of Gravity 26
 1. The Laws of Gravity
 2. Nichts, Nyet
 3. Kristallnacht
 4. A Last Dance
 5. You, Swimmer!
 6. For The Record
The first angels to arrive in the interior 31
The gods are changing face 32

Dawn, and your god has overreached 33
Metaphysical Geographies 34
Diabolus In Musica 37
Redshift 38
Precambrian 39
So many furious beams of light 40
The climbing child staggers 41
Old Song 42

III

Boreal Summer 45
Quiet 46
Glacial Lake Whitehorse 47
Spending Your Death In The Yukon 48
Local News 49
The Poet Divides His Time 51
A Canticle Of Ravens 53
Ice Fog 55
Stranded 56
Yukon Spring 57
Exile 59

I

Portraits Of A Lady

Our lady was forbidding, her babe,
grim. Even their clothes hung
rigid and absolute until Cimabue
and Giotto allowed air in. Then,

robes billowed to fall in gentle
waves. Campin invited us to hold
the child – as if it were our own –
and we grew nearly filial with

the mom. But the boy became a man
and died and she, after a proper
interval, danced off to vanish
in the wild. Boucher thought

he spied her there, bathing
with a friend. Later, Renoir may
have glimpsed her, naked at a bath.
Manet claimed to have found her

naked too, dining in some park
with two clothed men. This proved
a hoax. Pollock splashed through chaos
on his hopeless quest. Rothko sought

her. He disappeared and left us staring
at an empty field. We're abandoned
to our loss, victims who celebrate
an orphanhood. We do have that,

at least: a small meal, if not a feast,
a final bit of nourishment before
we stagger home (gullible, slack-
jawed, almost dumb) to beg the absolute
        to take us in.

What We Don't Yet Know About Uncles

If identical uncles
are presented with
identical circumstances,
say, a P-51 Mustang,

a draft-dodger nephew,
and the end of a century,
will molecules of anger
always be displaced

by death? How many
will remain to agitate
above the bodies and
how many will dissipate

into space after
the uncles are covered
by earth? How many atoms
of fury can bond

with one of love?
Are a nephew's first memories
part of a nation's traditions?
How does loss ionize

blood? Young uncles,
often in awe of an eldest,
are catalyzed from similar
structures, but an electron

is missing. Has it lost
the negative charge? Will it
be replaced in salt air
if a nephew is taken fishing?

Filialis

Father, I tried
to protect you from me,
read late
into The Book of Orphans.

I studied a child
who went west.
He entertained his captors
by drawing horses

on old newsprint
with charred sticks.
I fled west, then north
and north again

until I could lie down
drunk on snow. It was
February, midnight,
fifty below

when I dared sleep
to come at me. But
some voice with no body
woke me, shooed me home.

Body with no voice,
be patient with my life
of promises. Accept
this incomplete angel

your foolish son
carved in snow.

A Heritage

My father's name was Paul.
I don't give a damn
what anyone claims,
his name was Paul.

All those years,
while that other man
raised me, talking
of jackets and shoes

Paul hid in the forest
and gathered sticks.
No one knows if he
was building me a hut

or gathering fuel
for my fire.
He meant well,
as I do now,

dry and warm
stacking bones
and moss
for my daughter.

The Ash Lad

Mama and Papa and brothers,
Oscar and Peer,
have conned some befuddled sailor
out of a bottle of *Aquavit*.
They're all out stumbling
through the moonlight
while I curl by the hearth,
guarding our shack
and befriending
embers.

Outside, the wind screams …
or if it doesn't,
it should.
I am stirring coals
with Papa's favorite walking stick.

I'll be beaten, of course,
but no matter.
I feel lucky tonight
as if Gigantic Terror
were in the hen house
beheading the last of Peer's chickens,
and Terror's wife
were snorting around the root cellar
coveting jewels of which
Mama had only dreamt.

In the morning, Oscar's heart
may be found frozen
to the top of the woodpile.

If my family only knew
what luxury scraps of bread
and dry cheese were to me
they'd have me survive
on the herring
that grow in the forest
and on acorns
that wash ashore
after storms at sea.

For the moment,
there is nothing to lose
and nothing is fear.
Someday, however,
I am fated to marry a king's daughter
and live in splendor
down in Christiania.

No one there will box my ears.
With my "X" on parchment
I will transform ragamuffin cousins
into fat civil servants
and live out my days
ringing up tea
for an endless queue
of pastors.

Meanwhile,
crouched on a cliff
above my childhood village,
an ugly troll
blinded with tears
will be trapped
by sunrise.

On Vilano Bridge

Porpoises are rolling in Matanzas Bay.
Along the bridge Sunday crowds
sullenly jostle for room
to fish. I am too poor
to presume to wave at the huge
blue sail boats passing by.
I wish I hadn't lost everything.
An intense young woman on a bicycle
issues me a significant "good morning."
I think she is testing to see
if I'm just another one –
too wrapped up in my own small thoughts.
"Howdy" I say, but she
is already a hundred yards away
and has me pegged.

Better Than Nothing

Early morning, Salt Spring Island.
I am sitting on the dock
staring into the sound, my brain
sodden, weighted down
and sinking past the sense
of your parting words.

An aged schooner,
barely visible, anchored
in the mist
reminds me of Joseph Conrad
and of his men,
alone and hidden –
and then of you,
of course,
and the curiously erotic way
you have of keeping me
hungover and lonely
beside bodies of water
all over the continent.

From below, a jellyfish
arrests my thoughts.
I try to study
the perfect way
he executes his tasks,
pulsating, ingesting
and drifting.
No moods.
No traumas.
No brunettes.
I could sit here all day
with my indistinct awe. However,
I must rise and get back
to the full-time job
of living without you.

Whenever I See You Now, You're Laughing

for Patrick Lane

1970. Toronto. That winter
I quoted Sterne to anyone
who'd listen. "Gravity,
a mysterious carriage of the body
to conceal defects of the mind."
Introduced, I shook your hand
and offered wisdom from my 19 years:
"Your poems are too serious, too
gloomy." I don't remember what
you said – I think you simply
shook your head – but can recall
the sudden silence of that room.
In the quarter century since,
I've buried dogs with whisky prayers,
failed a wife, and stunned my daughter
when I fled. False to friends,
I was less shocked to learn
that they'd been false to me.
I have kept slash-fires burning late
to scare the bears and ghosts away
and helped to wreck Han hunting
grounds with the road we built.
I was the new guy on the green chain,
trembled, buckled, gave it up,
then begged again for work.
I have shoveled horse stalls
to keep sane, but
I don't throw stones.
I'm made of glass.

The Strait
for Raymond Carver

I walk beside the gray strait
and study on the far shore
Port Angeles, USA, where you
once walked and peered out
under the risen mist
at my beach in Canada.
One of these days
I will cross this tossed
water in my own boat,
visit your old house
with all my friends.
It can be a small boat.
I haven't been sober long
and have saved few friends
from my drunken storms,
just Dave and Greg.
Though I have some new friends:
Pat, Eve, Rhonda, John and Joan.
I love them as I love this strait
in a wind which sets all
the exotic ducks to rafting
beyond the breakers –
scoter, pintail, goldeneye –
yet launches the winter gulls.
They remind me of poems by
Wallace Stevens and Hart Crane.
But that's as far as I'll dare
love today. I won't be taking it
further, to some bar, won't
be dragging my love out,
swallow by drop, to the dregs.

Tomorrow, I'll set off from here
again, beside the strait, early
before the crowds,
with the gulls and poets
stride part-way
to wherever their metaphor
would take me.

Badlands Jesus

There was this big sad man.
He sat down beside me
on a train in Montana
late one November.

The month was gray and flat
and the land was. You couldn't tell
where the land gave off and the sky
began. It got so bad there
with the big sad man I couldn't tell
where his life gave off
and mine began.

He was that hurt.
You know the kind:
they have lost most everything
but their notebooks.
They carry around these thick spiral-bound notebooks
filled with their jottings
on Jesus

all this after "the wife" left, of course
taking the kids, and for good, of course

"On this page we find Jesus and my great hurt ...
Over here we have Jesus and the remnants
of my happiness ...

Jesus holds many surprises.
Jesus appears in myriad guises."

Jesus once appeared to the big sad man in a dream
but the sad man recognized Him not,
thought he was seeing a dead shaman
who beckoned him down
into that arroyo where
the rattlers hole up come winter.

He was commanded to cut in
on the secret dance
of old bones
and woke up terrified –
didn't know where his arroyo quit
and that bed began. This
somehow saved him
and he tried to save me

as I read the notebooks
as I tried to comfort him
as I missed the scenery
missed the deer and coyote

as my sobriety steadily failed.

Writing The Novel
for Eve

I must leave your grandmother
in Russia, alone in the snow
with the wolves.
I'm sorry.

I am not the one
to take her hand and lead her on
to England, to South Africa,
to Canada, finally.

Finally, only you can do that.
However, if I don't look back
directly, but only glance
back from the corner of my eye

I can glimpse the path
the two of you must take. And
on this quiet evening I can hear
a few faint bars

from some old song
the two of you must sing
to keep your spirits up
on the long journey.

I can't quite
make out the words,
but you will.

The Poet Attempts A Novel

My hero always fails me.
In Chapter One I give him everything:
height, youth, train fare,
a healthy mustache.
I encourage him to share
my family, my first wife,
the books I've read. All I ask
is that he be a man, push on
and meet his fate. But he
demands a rest at the first bend
we come to, and slumps there
as if brooding on the injustice
of it all: the noisy typewriter,
the stubby pencil.
I do my best, change
his name from Darryl to Erik,
Erik to Darryl. The pages pile up
but he never smiles and rarely
speaks. Other characters
wander by, take one look
and disappear. Alone
he leans against my second chapter
thinking only of himself,
his words, his crazy music.

Like Love

My friend is not here,
the friend who carries silver logs
for the fence, who
whistles the horses in
and whistles the horses
out, who knows all about
soft laughter and how
it must finally attend
all my missed marks.

She says, "Rest on this fence
beside the river and I will
describe your foolish talk
as something precious,
as something fine, like   .
an egg-shaped theory
about to evolve." Not once
have her numbers repeated
and we are further than
I have ever been to the right
of the decimal point
with no sign of rounding off.

        How many people
have I met
who have the power
to forgive someone
like me? Only one,
my friend who is not here,
who sets the heavy logs
for the fence perfectly parallel
to the coulee
where I hide.
She uses no tools, just
her bare hands,
and adjusts us
by ear.

The Exile House

This morning, lost again
I passed an old house
on a strange street
on my way home from the sea.
I suddenly craved to sit down
on its porch and wait
for someone to come to the door.
It was as if I had lived there before
and been happy.

Perhaps I waited too long
to tell someone about the old house
I wish I'd been raised in.
It was a huge dark thing
with many rooms
and a bright red porch
beneath a sky so gray, the clouds
could have blown in from 1952.

If I'd sat on that porch and waited
I might have had a day like no other.
A stranger might have soothed me or panicked.
Neighbors might have phoned the police.

I would have told them
that this is a house like the house
I should have grown up in, that
it was a huge dark thing
with many rooms. The neighbors
had feared the very idea of it, feared me
and barred me from school.

My only friends
were the ancient revolutionaries
who hid in the rooms.
They called me Little Shadow
and told me stories in their many
old tongues. They are dead now
and I've read too many books.

II

The Death of Saint-Denys Garneau

The heart fires off a line
                    that won't scan, then, ellipsis

The brain slowly quits its attempt
                    to count the cadence of silence

There is only one river, a gray page of evening
                    punctuated by tiny fish

He spins, seeking the path with no ends
                    then drifts off into a forest

as if Orpheus, by giving up his impossible art,
                    could be free

NOTE: *Hector de Saint-Denys Garneau (1912-1943) was a French Canadian poet, devastated by the publication of his own first book — he felt he had somehow betrayed himself. He died of a heart attack beside a river not far from a cabin he was building.*

Sedimentary

this old hand falls
short of the memory rock

short of the sharps
short of the flats

settles finally, more loved
less perfected

where sprigs of wild sage
grasp at loess
and a hot wind
curries bone

Here, Now

Of course, you believe I am overreacting
again, that what I heard was only a moth
colliding with the sea, a fish beating
against the sky, night getting into the garden

again. I tell you, what I saw was a girl
dragging a thin finger across wet paint,
erasing a nipple, smudging the sun, blurring
that scarlet line, the horizon

which once could prevent white earth
from falling into the white sky.
Have you never met a child
given to fevers contracted from books?

I read where it says,
    winter is past.
I read where it says,
    the rain is over, is gone.
I read where
    flowers appear on earth.

Now, you read where it says,
the voice of the flower says
cry

The Laws of Gravity

For Paul Celan

1. *The Laws of Gravity*

It takes longer to understand his poems
than it took a Luger's bullet
to drop from his mother's skull

longer that it took
an old rabbi to grow quiet
and settle into the ice

longer than it took a many-hued shroud
to unravel and assume
the odor of earth

longer than it took two lungs
to fill with water

longer than it takes
to survive

2. *Nichts, Nyet*

Celan sits,

                no, slumps

    in the dark
in the audience and studies his hand,
the hand he was meant to write poems with.
The wrist is swollen and the fingers
torn by the rocks he carries
creating new order
from old chaos.
On stage
beloved Ruth performs

the one play
liberators will allow.
Her familiar body spells out
its simple message: *Genius*
resides at the base of the thumb,
wisdom in the wrist.
There is only so much we need to know
and we will know it all
come curtain fall
when we'll rush to our barracks
and beg for sleep. Our rocks
wake us early.
He gets so he understands
the needs of rocks,
gets so he can sing
like a stone.
The critics are furious!
"Is this some child
to think
a warm hand
might hatch
a rock?
Nothing he suffers
buys him that right,
to speak for a stone.
The people.
The people must know,
rocks we stack into a wall.
Stones we throw."

3. Kristallnacht

You spoke Rumanian, Russian, French, English,
but sang in a tongue of sharpened wire
for those who had no ears
to hear

all language become the one
proclaimed by that strong angel,
trumpeted by those beasts
full of wide eyes within

Giving honor, giving glory
shouting HOLY, holy, holy
(resting not) day and night,
day, and most especially, night

above the crashing of that glass sea

4. *A Last Dance*

Celan and his friends never could
discover the evil chord
that lurks in the works
of Mozart, those notes
that will not serve
the people

but there is always someone who can. No
night is so dark it will blanket
the pleasure of young Jews
keeping warm at a clandestine piano.

For a metronome we have always
that knock at the door.

If you forget the shibboleth
hum
                to the tune of basalt.

Whistle up lignite.

Fill your pockets with stone.

                    Quickly now,

this way to the river!

5. *You, Swimmer!*

It is He who made us, and not
we ourselves. Isn't that right, Paul?

But anyone can unmake us,
any dumb beast with a gun

and we can unmake ourselves
any middle-aged poet
with a river

can
to a certain extent, though
a murdered mother might outlast us,
assume our form
and walk

               And that's why
it is always safer to sleep in a crib
than a bed.

You didn't exchange your crib
for a bed
until you were twelve,
but why stop then? Why
not twenty or fifty or
three score and ten?

Sooner or later,
all sleeping adults must toss
turn, scream
silently
and fall.

The poet wakes
before he hits.

Let the floods clap their hands
to receive him.

6.   For The Record

Paul Antschel
shall have no
name in the
Street of Exile

Paul Ancel
shall be driven
from darkness
into light

Paul Celan
shall leap out
of this world
at the end

of taking on
names: Anonymous
Word Angel

The first angels to arrive in the

The first angels to arrive in the interior
were blown here from the coast
like exhausted gulls by a gale.

Dirty and lost, they recalled
only that they had hoped
to test man and tax him

– as they'd been invited to do
for those most mistaken
folk of the plains.

So this is how insomnia arrived
in the mountains. This is why,
during these back-country

summer nights, we stand up
one by one to wander the forest
where we collect our bouquets

of weeds and twigs and thorns.
And this is why, come dawn,
we are always so desperate

to drink any brew
that might dilute
a taste of salt in the wind.

The gods are changing face

The gods are changing face
again: He gods, She gods,
Goat gods, all the vast hierarchy
including the One and Only.

Sloughed off, a huge dry grin
drops. The down-rush of wind
staggers all before it; women
stagger cursing into men.

Blacks cast charred fur
against the gale. Whites stumble
after burnt feathers. Day bursts.
An old forgotten night comes on.

Gibbering, we scurry back
onto familiar branches
while down below
lead-faced messengers

and spies with granite wings
form up awkward squadrons
            by the light
            of burning books.

Dawn, and your god has overreached

Dawn, and your god has overreached
   again, juxtaposed the improbable:
summer sun, bird song, and absence,
   some flesh made word.

You open your eyes to chaos
   like a child who has been blind-
folded and spun by sleep. Miscues
   are canticled from corners.

How pale you've grown
   while feeling around in the dark
for a home.

So stumble now, out into day.
   Once again, man is separated
from beast by laughter.

Metaphysical Geographies

contemplatio in caligine divina

1.

Anything can be sung

fused, lobbed

the chorus can echo any blast
and sway

robes billowing
in each aftershock

2.

We once sucked sweet oil
from flinty rock, honey
from stone

We wander now, eyes
cast down
mewling for a second gift
of carbon

3.

Beware this frontier
its harsh face
broken
into promise
the lichen-splashed
rock glacier
but briefly
reposed

4.

Trumpeted

breathless

over the lip

into some valley of vision

each of us

flung

onto a cold canvas air

5.
"Ye shall speak into air."

finger
breaks in upon finger
that failing grip
dear old gesture
orphaned

6.
When the hymn forgets
its words

God listens

His variables
gone forth
multiplied

coda

When only the ineffable remains
you abandon your witless
vocables, leap
free from all kneeling
so quickly
a black beam
shatters

behind the eyes

Now,
you must feel your way
along the cold
wall

Fingers trace this journey
in a frost that cracks rocks, ends
meaning, pre-
maturely.

The punch line falls away
drags you
in after it
writing

Diabolus In Musica
for Edwin Hubble

Through the night
I sift our *wild abyss*
for the note
find
this one and
that one and
maybe
one other
Come dawn
thrilled
I connect these dots
and stumble. Listen
to our universe scrape
against that other
slate upon slate
Fissure
bisects sphere
Sullen angel
collides
with sullen angel
We are, all of us,
stunned
by the patterns of ruin
Launched into this noise
silence soars
joyous
and false
like the whistling of one
who would have us

Redshift

for John Scofield

Your hand appears, is blue
a blur

then steadies itself
against cool pale wood.

Only now,
may your fingers stretch,
yearning toward that red ebullience,

that final planet.

The search begins with your guitar.

Precambrian

Consider the far south's old stones,
the dignity of rocks
with a heritage of billions.

Here, in our north, we may peer
back only by some millions
and everywhere we step

we mar the loess. Meanwhile,
at the antipodes, rocks
maintain a steady dialogue

with stars, speak
as zircon and agate,
triumphant words

and polished
untainted by
the brevity of thirst.

So many furious beams of light

So many furious beams of light
dissolve those shadows
we grew up with.

Now, each of us rises in heat,
in horror, pistons to drive
our great engine art

deep into the dark.
As ever, some distant surface
promises traction

and a cool place
where words might keep
well beyond us

but, when we approach,
deep depressions
resolve into fossil:

prints of the paws
of those who failed
here before us.

The climbing child staggers

The climbing child staggers,
stops, baffled. Who
has recalled the warm light

that had just been his –
reflected from the face
of this sandstone hill?

And who, suddenly,
has intercepted
a scent of sage

from the single triumphant sprig
that may yet cling
to memory-blasted rock?

Old Song

Everyone can love a dry
cold, a dry heat, a dry
eye in the house

it's such easy fortitude
such easy go easy
go

meanwhile, the quaking aspen
are quaking again
and it's only September

all of us are chilled
all of us
all the way home

III

Boreal Summer

I wish to register my concern,
my distress, with this
annual suppression of darkness,
this revocation

of our right to stars. How
are we to locate ourselves
if we look up, only to discover
a few blood-stained clouds

in our sky? What's a little blood
to hydrogen? Each year,
we are misplaced. Believe me,
all that terrified tramps have cried

while stumbling in their circles
is true. By August, I am spinning
alone in the forest, trying
to summon faith, whistling

my tired air: *a sense of place*, just
another aging professional
at the peak of his career,
his season, his one day to mate.

Quiet

A recent study has revealed
elderly men are dying alone
in shacks in the forest.

They have sickened and slipped
through cracks in quartz
and timber, down

through woodsmoke and frost,
deep into the domain
of ancient wool.

They arrived here early
in the century, strong and thirsty.
They packed in accordions,

harmonicas, guitars ...
then quickly became geniuses
of kerosene, cordwood and coal.

They are said to have sung
that last generation of wolves
            to its rest.

Glacial Lake Whitehorse

At last, reprieved
by melting ice
an ancient lake fled
down our valley to the sea
        and never returned.

Without fish, sterile,
all its waters ever knew
was wind.

Tonight, a dry wind
cries out for waves again.

Spending Your Death In The Yukon

If the winter nights up here
are perfect for ghost watching
they are even more perfect
for being a ghost.

Imagine a soul – by day
it felt unclaimed and gray –
suddenly set aglow
by a bombardment of northern lights.

Then, picture that scene framed
by the leafless willows, encrusted
with hoarfrost.
They make good company,
                    like the ghosts of trees.

And the moon! The moon over all
this snow is so bright
even a shade would cast a shadow.

Local News

For the past week,
an exhausted young minister
has been locked away
in the back of the hospital
by his friend, the doctor.
All summer, young men of this town
have been taking their own lives
as if preparing for winter.
During each last breath,
the minister was catching his.

He barely had time to console
a wife, a father or mother
before being called off
by another disaster.
Every loud noise made him jump,
each splash in the river.
He lay awake entire nights
listening to hemp being coiled
on the far side of the world
in preparation
for his next failure.

Staid townsfolk complain
that their holy man consorts
with the loose and the addled.
The response seems so obvious
the doctor doesn't share it
with his sedated friend.
He whispers simply, "Hush for now.
Tomorrow, it may end."

Meanwhile, in some alley of that town,
a jug of cheap wine accompanies
a young man's brain into middle age.
His childhood friends
run in terror from his rage
so he wanders alone
and slack-jawed until dawn
when he'll steal a shotgun
and vanish to the poplars.

The young minister calls out
from his sleep.

The Poet Divides His Time

I love too well
the place I've just come from
to ever be truly happy.
Twice this winter, I've picked up
and flown south. Twice
this winter, I've flown back again,
each time for good
and always.

Budweiser and shrimp.
    Heidelberg and moose.
Bourbon and lobster.
    Rye and grayling –

always the overpowering appetite
for the bounty of wherever I'm not.

This afternoon, I looked out
of the kitchen window
at Dawson City's snow-covered
Moosehide rock slide
and considered for a moment the myth
of the Indians who were trapped there
by an angry god, then
shook my head at myself
for being within sight of it
                                again.

Wherever I go, I always come back here,
even from beautiful St. Augustine,
with its pirate-haunted narrow streets,
pelicans, margaritas and
aggressive women on the beach.

Friends in both towns shake their heads.
Bartenders in both towns greet me
the same way: "Hey, whaddya doin' here?
We thought you'd left!"

I make blushing confused explanations.

From St. Augustine I return
through Toronto, Winnipeg, Whitehorse
to Dawson City and home
with its spruce hills, two rivers
and the bar where I sit like some fixture
that's forever being sent out for repairs.

A Canticle of Ravens

All winter, ravens
have been hopping
from failed poem
to failed poem
as if wanting
to take over
and write
one of their own:

Ravens of creation
Ravens of death
Ravens of wisdom
Ravens of hilarity
Ravens of filth
Ravens perched upon mounds of frozen shit
on deserted streets
beneath a burning cold pink sky
after the best years of your life
have passed you by
and you are so lonely
pride fails you who
act overjoyed to see them.

Ravens

are the patrons
of our least comforting humanities.
They joke with wolves,
but torment dogs.
Calm science cannot
contain them.
We can label them
Corvus corax
until we're blue, but

Corvus corax
when chanted in sorrow
until the spring thaw
becomes a curse
which turns back
to charm the chanter,
        some careless father:

Daddy has gone a hunting

and a multitude of black–
feathered landlords
surrounds that unlit shack.
They squawk in tongues
to make impossible demands
upon his little daughter.

She wrings her ancient hands.
Daddy is never coming back.

Ice Fog

We are the people
in God's belly.
He exists in all directions,
infinite and gray.

There can be no world beyond
the crystals we drift among.
Only heretics hearken to sounds
other than the scream of boots
on frozen ground.

Once, we may have known words
for the many shades
of absence,
but through endless winter
have forgotten speech.

How foolish to imagine
lights in a sky
or the heat of lives
beyond the reach
of our numb hands.

Stranded

Memory causes the compass of the heart
to spin in all creatures
who chose to forsake water
for dry land.

Remind me again: a creek
leads to a river. A river
leads to the sea. I was calm
once beside the sea.

Today, past and present met
upon the ice of the Yukon River.
The February sun nearly blinded me.

That same sun once lured us up
and called us out – slow, awkward,
laughable miracles, dazzled by flowers.

Yukon Spring

Now that the snow has been beaten
back into small dour patches
between the black spruce,
I cannot sit still.
Each morning finds me
out hiking beneath
the new sun,
striding purposefully
as if I had somewhere
to go.

There seems to be a small
inarticulate religious fanatic
inside me. I must bear him
with me whenever I go
along the river and up
into the hills.
He makes me hum
some freighted tune
and I feel like an anonymous
composer of hymns
might have felt
long ago
in some Old World forest
with the latest plague
at his heels.

Some days, however,
I discover myself to be
exactly where I am,
lost upon a slim trail
in the Yukon
but shorter

and darker
and stronger
and carrying a burden
of still-warm flesh
across my shoulders
while making soft sounds
deep in my throat
of thanksgiving
and praise
and hunger
as night
races me home.

Exile

Again I have summoned the word
exile. How many decades must I waste
at laments before coming to believe
my long exile has ended, is served?
True, it is cold here at the northern-
most frontier of my wandering. Winter
has arrived with October. Last night,
I heard geese taking their leave.
This morning, trumpeter swans deserted
at first light. Was the map too simple
to comprehend? My final memory
of the South is surely distorted
by some recent adventure in this land.
A slow summer walk with Elizabeth
among huge oaks has become
a quick hike with Patricia
through yellowing poplar.
I have confused magpies with mocking birds
and river willow with sumac too long.
What I recall as endless possibility
was just a young man's boasting
and greed. I will indulge myself
with no further talk of promise.
I was called to walk this high place.
Around me lies all the bounty
one could ever hope to spend,
a home hidden only by snow.